THE WORLD'S BEST GOLF JOKES

by Russ Edwards
and Jack Kreismer

RED-LETTER PRESS, INC.
SADDLE RIVER, NEW JERSEY

ACKNOWLEDGMENTS

Project Development Coordinator:
Kobus Reyneke

Cover design and typography:
s.w.artz, inc.

INTRODUCTION

Golfers claim that the game offers good exercise and that certainly is true – at least for the caddies. It seems many players confuse getting fit with throwing one. After riding around in a golf cart all day, many times the only thing a golfer exercises is his elbow at the Nineteenth Hole. Now, with **THE WORLD'S BEST GOLF JOKES**, the duffer can give his diaphragm a good workout, too, with hilarious golf stories that will have his golfing buddies laughing with him instead of at him.

THE WORLD'S BEST GOLF JOKES

MR. JOKES

Wisecracks for Wiseguys

A couple of guys are standing around the water cooler Monday morning when one says, "What'd you do this weekend?"

"Dropped hooks in the water."

"Went fishing, eh?"

"No, golfing."

I got my dad one of those typical Father's Days cards. You know, with a picture of a hunting coat hanging on a peg, a duck decoy, and some golf clubs leaning in the corner. Perfect card for him, because there's nothing Dad loves more than going out in the woods on a frosty morning and beating ducks to death with a four-iron.

-DANIEL LIEBERT

I wish my name was Tom Kite.

-IAN BAKER-FINCH, ON SIGNING AUTOGRAPHS

A pair of duffers are waiting their turn on the tee, when a drop-dead gorgeous woman in her birthday suit runs across the fairway and into the woods. Two men in white coats, and another guy carrying two buckets of sand are chasing after her, and a little old man is bringing up the rear.

"What the heck is going on here?" one of the golfers asks the old geezer.

He says, "She's a nymphomaniac from the funny farm. She keeps trying to escape from the asylum and us attendants are trying to catch her."

The golfer says, "What about that guy with the buckets of sand?"

"Oh, him. That's his handicap. He caught her last time."

Doctor Dudley, toting his golf bag, was heading out of his dentist's office when his receptionist said,

"Doctor, I have Mr. Arnold on the line. He has a toothache."

Dudley answered, "Tell him to call back tomorrow. I've got eighteen cavities to fill today."

If you're stupid enough to whiff, you should be smart enough to forget it.

-Arnold Palmer

Around the clubhouse they'll tell you even God has to practice his putting. In fact, even Nicklaus does.

-JIM MURRAY

*Golf is a game where the ball always lies
poorly and the player always lies well.*

-ANONYMOUS

"obSIRvations"

Two things that ain't long for this world
- dogs that chase cars and professional
golfers who chip for pars.

-Lee Trevino

A golfer sliced his ball right off the course, hitting a lawyer who was walking down a nearby sidewalk.

The golfer ran over to the stricken lawyer to see if he was all right.

"Im going to sue you for five thousand dollars," the lawyer said.

"I'm awfully sorry but I yelled 'Fore!'"

"I'll take it!" the lawyer said.

A panic-stricken golfer charged into the clubhouse, grabbed the pro by the arm and said, "You gotta help! I was on the ninth hole and hit a terrible slice. The ball sailed right off the course and hit a guy riding a motorcycle. He lost control and swerved into the path of a truck. The truck tried to stop but jack-knifed, rolled over and broke apart. It was carrying thousands of bee hives and now the bees are attacking everyone in sight. It's awful! It's a disaster! What should I do?"

The pro answered, "Well, the first thing is you've got to keep your arms straight and remember to get your right hand a bit more under the club ..."

I went to play golf and tried to shoot my age, but I shot my weight instead.

-BOB HOPE

Golf is one of the few sports where a white man can dress like a black pimp.

-ROBIN WILLIAMS

The drill sergeant decides to play a late afternoon-early evening game of golf and hooks up to play a twosome.

Four quadruple bogeys, three triple bogeys and two double bogeys later the sarge's partner says, "When did you take up this game?"

The drill sergeant says, "Nineteen fifty-nine."

"Nineteen fifty-nine?" says the other golfer. "I would think that you'd be able to play a little better than this."

"Whaddya mean?" says the sarge. "It's only twenty-two thirteen right now."

A golfer goes to a psychiatrist and says, "My wife thinks I'm crazy because I like plaid golf socks."

"That's not so strange," replies the doctor. "As a matter of fact, I kind of like them, too."

"Really?" exclaimed the patient, excited to find a sympathetic ear. "Do you like yours with chocolate fudge or Hollandaise sauce?"

Golf is a game in which you yell fore, shoot six, and write down five.

-Paul Harvey

I play golf even though I hate it. I'm not done with the game yet. I hate those windmills.

-MARK GUIDO

A politician died and, as might be expected, he went straight to Hell. As Satan was showing him around the place, he noticed a beautiful golf course that would put Augusta to shame. Being a lifelong golf fanatic, he was thrilled. Striding into the pro shop, he spotted a sign that read, "Only The Finest Equipment And All Absolutely Free - Help Yourself."

Having selected a fantastic set of matched clubs and a first class golf bag, he next needed a caddy. The caddy shack was filled with gorgeous women who were movie stars in life. He chose Marilyn Monroe who was wearing a teddy. He couldn't wait to begin his dream game! As he stepped up to the tee, he reached into the ball pocket and found it empty. He looked up to see Satan grinning from ear to ear.

"Don't bother going back to the pro shop. There aren't any balls anywhere - you see, that's the Hell of it."

A duffer walks into the nineteenth hole, orders three stiff ones and downs them immediately, then starts sobbing uncontrollably.

The bartender says, "Hey, buddy, calm down. What's the matter?"

"My wife just left me for my golfing partner," he sobs.

"That's okay. Take it easy. There are plenty of other fish in the sea," says bartender.

"I'm not worried about that," the duffer cries, "but he's the only one I could ever beat."

How come the white male politicians who vote against affirmative action are always so willing to accept a handicap on the golf course?

-PAUL KRASSNER

Golfers find it a very trying matter to turn at the waist, particularly if they have a lot of waist to turn.

-HARRY VARDON

Q: *What's it called when you purchase a set of clubs at list price?*

A: *Getting shafted.*

~~~~

Q: *Who was the top golfer in North Africa?*

A: *Gene Saharazen.*

~~~~

Q: *How can you tell the golfers in church?*

A: *They're the ones who pray with the interlocking grip.*

A guy was stranded on an island for ages. One day as he was walking on the beach, a beautiful woman in a wet suit emerges from the surf.

"Hey, cutie pie. Have you been here long?" she asks.

"I reckon about ten years."

"Do you smoke?"

"Oh, what I'd do for a cigarette!" he responds.

With that, she unzips a pocket in the sleeve of her wet suit, pulls out a pack of cigarettes, lights one and gives it to him.

"I guess it's been a long while since you've had a drink, huh?"

"You got that right," he says.

She pulls out a flask from another pocket, gives it to him and he takes a swig.

"I bet you haven't played around in a while either," she coos as she begins to unzip the front of her wet suit.

Wide-eyed, he says, "Don't tell me you have a set of golf clubs in there too!?"

On a blistering day in south Florida, a priest, a minister and a rabbi were playing golf alongside beautiful Biscayne Bay. As the mercury climbed past 90, 95 and then topped 100 degrees, the men of cloth couldn't take it any longer. The bay looked so inviting that they decided to strip down and jump in the water.

After frolicking and splashing about for a while, they figured that they'd cooled down enough to get back to their game.

Before they could dress, a foursome of lady golfers appeared nearby. The minister and priest covered their private parts in a panic but the rabbi just covered his face. After the women passed by, the priest and minister asked the rabbi why he covered his face instead of his privates.

As the rabbi fastened the last button to his shirt, he replied, "Listen, I don't know about you, but in my congregation it's the face they'll recognize."

A lawyer mailed a note to his client:

"Dear Mr. Foxworth: Thought I saw you at the nineteenth hole yesterday... Went over to your table to say hello, but it wasn't you so I went back.

One twentieth of an hour: $20."

"obSIRvations"

The only problem with the Senior Tour is that when you're through here, they put you in a box.

-J.C. Snead

Learning to play golf is like learning to play the violin. It's not only difficult to do, it's very painful to everyone around you.

-HAL LINDEN

I deny allegations by Bob Hope that during my last game I hit an eagle, a birdie, an elk, and a moose.

-PRESIDENT GERALD FORD

At the Sleepy Hollow golf course, a foursome approached the 11th tee where the fairway runs along the edge of the course and adjoins a highway.

Forrester teed off and sliced the ball right over the fence. It hit the front tire of a bus and bounced back onto the green and into the cup for a hole-in-one.

"How on earth did you ever get it to bounce off that bus?" asked one of his astonished buddies.

"Well, first off," he replied, "you've got to know the schedule."

Rex had a particularly bad day on the course. Nothing went right and by the time he missed a two-foot putt on the 17th to round his score up to 130, he blew his stack.

He removed his golf clubs from his bag and cracked them over his knees before hurling them into the water.

"I'll never play golf again," he roared.

He then kicked the bag around, tossed that in the water too and, in a super-human burst of rage, he flipped the golf cart over into the lake. At that point, he stomped off toward the clubhouse.

One of the members happened by, just missing the tantrum and innocently asked, "Hey Rex, we need a fourth for tomorrow. Can you make it?"

Rex stopped in his tracks, looked up and said, "What time?"

*What's so nice about our tours is that you
can't remember your bad shots.*

-BOBBY BRUE, ON THE SENIOR CIRCUIT

Harry loved golf more than anything but as he got
into his 80's his eyesight began to fail him.

Commiserating about his problem at the nineteenth
hole, he met Louie, another octogenarian who lived
for golf and, although he had perfect eyesight, was
crippled by arthritis. They decided to join forces and
play a round the next morning. Harry teed off and
the ball hooked a wee bit but landed not too far left
of the green.

"Hey, that felt good, Louie. Did you see where
the ball went?"

"Sure did," replied Louie.

"So where'd it land?"

Louie scratched his head and replied, "I forget."

The Sheik of all sheiks was rushed to the hospital for an emergency appendectomy. The attending surgeon expertly removed the organ despite serious complications.

"You saved my life," said the Sheik upon regaining consciousness. "Anything you want is yours."

"That's not necessary," responded the doctor.

"But I insist," said the Sheik.

"Well, okay, I could use a new set of matched clubs."

"Done!" said the Sheik.

A few weeks went by and the busy doctor had forgotten all about the Sheik's promise when a fax arrived. It read: From: The Sheik To: The Good Doctor…I have bought you the new set of golf clubs you requested but am eternally embarrassed and humbled that they sadly do not match. I was appalled to discover that four do not have swimming pools.

*I'm an ordinary sort of fellow - 42 around
the chest, 42 around the waist, 96 around
the golf course, and a nuisance around
the house.*

-GROUCHO MARX

An executive who often left to play golf during
business hours told his secretary to advise all callers
that he was away from his desk. A golfer who was
part of the executive's foursome forgot where they
were playing on this particular day so he called the
secretary. Loyal to a fault, she'd only say that her
boss was away from his desk.

Finally, the exasperated golfer said, "Look, just
tell me. Is he five miles or ten miles away from
his desk?"

A small private plane was flying over southwest Florida when all of a sudden the engine died, miles away from any airport. The pilot turned to his wife and said, "Don't worry honey, there're dozens of golf courses in this area. I'll just land on the next one I see."

To which his wife replied, "What do you mean 'don't worry'? I've seen you play. You'll never hit the fairway!"

Ninety percent of putts that are short don't go in.

-Yogi Berra

Golf scores are directly proportionate to the number of witnesses.

-ANONYMOUS

A minister and his very conservative wife had a great marriage except for his long business trips and lifelong obsession with golf.

One day while he was away, she was cleaning and found a box of mementos in the back of the bedroom closet. In it she found three golf balls and $800.

That night when he called, she asked him the meaning of the three golf balls. He said, "Well, dear I've been keeping that box for twenty years. I'm ashamed to admit it but so great is my passion for the game of golf that occasionally I swear on the course. Every time I use unsavory language, I penalize myself one golf ball."

Shocked that her husband, a man of the cloth, would ever use four-letter words, the wife was at first taken aback but then thought, "Well, three balls means that he's only cursed three times in 20 years. I suppose that isn't so bad."

"All right dear," she said, "I forgive you for your lapses, but tell me, what's the $800 for?"

"Oh that," answered the minister. "I found a guy who buys golf balls at two bucks a dozen."

At a hoity toity country club which strictly enforces its rules, a member saw a guest of the club place his ball five inches in front of the tee markers. The member hurriedly went over to the guest and said, "Sir, I don't know whether you've ever played here before, but we have very stringent rules about placing your tee at or behind the markers before driving the ball."

The guest looked the snooty club member right in the eye and retorted, "First, I've never played here before. Second," he added, "I don't care about your rules. And third, this is my second shot."

My family was so poor they couldn't afford me. The lady next door had me.

-LEE TREVINO

Titleist has offered me a big contract
not to play its balls.

-BOB HOPE

A husband and wife, both golf fanatics, were discussing the future as they sat by a warm fireplace. "Dear," the wife said, "if I died would you remarry?"

"Well, if something were to happen to you in the near future, I guess so. After all, we're not exactly senior citizens."

"Would you live in this house with her?" the wife asked.

"I would think so."

She continued, "How about my car? Would she get that?"

"I don't see why not."

"What about my golf clubs? Would you give them to her too?"

"Heck, no" the husband exclaimed. "She's left-handed."

Q: *What do hackers and condemned playgrounds have in common?*

A: *Lousy swings.*

~~~~

Q: *How is a wedding ring like a bag of golf clubs?*

A: *They are both instruments of eternal servitude.*

"obSIRvations"

They call it golf because all of the other four-letter words were taken.

-Raymond Floyd

Golf practice - something you do to convert a nasty hook into a wicked slice.

-HENRY BEARD

*If you really want to get better at golf, go
back and take it up at a much earlier age.*

-THOMAS MULLIGAN

A terrible golfer hits a ball into a gigantic
bunker. He asks his caddie, "What club should
I use now?"

The caddie says, "The club isn't the important
thing. Just make sure to take along plenty of food
and water."

Did you hear the one about the pub for vulgar golfers?
It's called Par For The Coarse.

A duffer sliced his tee shot right into the woods. Rather than take a penalty, he decided to go for it. Unfortunately, his second shot caromed right off the trunk of a big old oak tree, hitting him right between the eyes and killing him instantly.

The next thing he knew, he was standing before St. Peter at the Pearly Gates.

St. Peter, trying to find his name on the list, said, "Oh, here it is. But according to this, you're not scheduled to die for another 25 years. How did you get here?

"In two."

Mulligan: invented by an Irishman who wanted to hit one more 20-yard grounder.

-JIM BISHOP

Goldfarb died and left no family but he did leave dozens of golfing buddies. At the service, Schaffer, one of his best friends, came up to the coffin and placed an envelope full of cash in it.

"Goldie, I've owed you this thousand dollars far too long. I wanted to make sure I paid off my golfing bet."

A few moments later, Anderson, another golf crony, placed an envelope of cash in the coffin and said, "Here's that golf bet payoff from last summer. Now we're even."

Later on, after everyone had been to the cemetery, the guys decided to hoist a few in Goldfarb's memory at the nineteenth hole. At one point, Schaffer and Anderson approached McCoy who, by that time, was feeling no pain.

"We were wondering," said Schaffer, "did you get around to paying Goldfarb that $1,500 you owed him?"

"I certainly did," replied McCoy. "When I went up to the casket, I put it in."

"That was decent of you," said Anderson.
"That coffin certainly had an awful lot of money in it."

"That concerned me too," said McCoy. *"That's why, when I went up there, I took out the envelopes that had $2,000 in them and threw in a check for $3,500."*

One lesson you better learn if you want to be in politics is that you never go out and beat the president.

-President Lyndon B. Johnson

A driving range is the place where golfers go to get all the good shots out of their system.

-HENRY BEARD

*I hit two fairways - well, maybe four, but
only two I was aiming at.*

-JOHN DALY

A terribly slow-playing golfer was getting heat from his caddy all afternoon when he finally lost his cool. "I've had enough of your snide remarks. When we get back to the clubhouse, I'll see that you no longer have any work here."

"You gotta be kidding," said the caddy. "By the time we get there, I'll be retired."

Maybe you've heard why clergymen play such poor golf... They don't have the vocabulary for it.

Arnold Palmer and Tiger Woods were playing the fourteenth hole when Tiger's tee shot landed behind a huge 75-foot sycamore tree. Tiger looked at Arnie and said, "How would you play this one? Lay up and take an extra stroke?"

Arnie replied, "When I was your age, I'd just play right over the tree."

Tiger, not wanting to be shown up by the old master, proceeded to hit the ball high, but not high enough. It bounced off the tree and dropped out of bounds. Tiger, really ticked at this point, asked, "Arnie, how did you ever hit a ball over that tree?"

Arnie replied, "Well, when I was your age, that tree was only three feet tall."

The more you play golf, the less you know about it.

-PATTY BERG

I used to want to shoot my age. Now I
would just like to shoot my temperature.

-JERRY FELICIOTTO

A retiree was given a set of golf clubs by his co-workers. Thinking he'd try the game, he asked the local pro for lessons, explaining that he knew nothing whatever of the sport.

The pro showed him the stance and swing, then said, "Just hit the ball toward the flag on the first green."

The novice teed up and smacked the ball straight down the fairway and onto the green where it stopped inches from the hole.

"Now what?" the fellow asked the speechless pro.

After he was able to speak again the pro finally said, "Uh, you're supposed to hit the ball into the cup."

The beginner responded, "Oh, great! Now you tell me!"

Four old duffers had a Saturday morning 8 o'clock tee time for years. On one such morning, they noticed a guy watching them as they teed off. At every tee, he caught up with them and had to wait.

When they reached the fifth tee, the guy walked up to the foursome and handed them a card which read, "I am deaf and mute. May I play through?"

The old duffers were outraged and signaled to him that nobody plays through their group. He'd just have to bide his time.

On the eighth hole, one of the foursome was in the fairway lining up his second shot. All of the sudden he got bopped in the back of the head by the tremendous force of a golf ball. He turned around and looked back at the tee. There stood the deaf mute, frantically waving his arm in the air, holding up four fingers.

A real fire-and-brimstone fundamentalist preacher always made it a point to admonish his flock about playing golf on the Sabbath. But, alas, one springtime Sunday morning the preacher himself was tempted to play a quick round. Up in Heaven, the angel in charge of such things, Melrose, spotted the minister and was outraged at his hypocrisy. Melrose went to see the Big Guy and told him of the reverend's transgression.

"I agree he should be punished," said God. "I'll take care of it."

With that, back down on the course, the preacher stepped up to the tee and hit the ball perfectly. It sailed down the fairway, cleared all the hazards, plopped down on the green and rolled gently into the cup for an ace. Melrose was flabbergasted. "A hole-in-one? I thought you were going to punish him."

"I did," God replied. "Who's he going to tell?"

A golf club walks into a bar and asks for a beer. The bartender refuses to serve him.

"Why not?" demands the golf club.

"Because you'll be driving later."

A golf ball is like a clock. Always hit it at six o'clock and make it go toward twelve o'clock. But make sure you're in the same time zone.

-Chi Chi Rodriguez

A professional will tell you the amount of flex you need in the shaft of your clubs. The more the flex, the more strength you will need to break the thing over your knees.

-STEPHEN BAKER

I'm hitting the woods just great, but I'm having a helluva time gettin' out of them.

                      -HENRY TOSCANO

Q: What are the four worst words you could hear during a game of golf?

A: "It's still your turn!"

Phone conversation at the nineteenth hole:

"Hello, Fairleigh Golf Club."

"I'd like to find out if my husband is there."

"No ma'am."

"You haven't even heard my name. How can you possibly know he isn't there?"

"Because ma'am, no husband is ever here when his wife calls."

Old Findley finally went to that big golf course in the sky, leaving an estate of $200,000. After all his final expenses were paid at the funeral home, his widow confided to her closest friend that there was nothing left.

"Nothing?" the woman asked incredulously. "How can that be? You said he had $200,000."

"Well," replied the widow Findley, "the funeral cost $8,000 and there was the matter of $2,000 back dues at the country club. The rest went for the memorial stone."

"$190,000 for a memorial stone! That's unbelievable. How big was it?"

The widow smiled and sighed, "Oh, just over seven carats."

Nothing dissects a man in public quite like golf.

-BRENT MUSBERGER

I'd give up golf if I didn't have so many sweaters.

-BOB HOPE

Hank the hack was having his usual day on the links, hitting into the woods, losing balls and, in general, making his caddy's job horrible. On the fifteenth, he approached the ball in the fairway and hollered at the caddy to give him a three-wood.

"Uh, excuse me," the caddy began to say.

"Just be quiet and give me the three-wood," Hank demanded.

The caddy gave it to him and watched. Hank then hit a beautiful shot that bounced once on the fairway, then onto the green and into the cup for a 1 under. "You see that," said Hank, "I know what I'm doin', kid."

"Heckuva shot, sir," said the exasperated caddy. "It's just a shame it wasn't your ball."

Do pediatricians play miniature golf on Wednesdays?

Golf is a game whose aim is to hit a
very small ball into an even smaller
hole with weapons singularly ill-
designed for the purpose.

-*Sir Winston Churchill*

I retired from competition at twenty-eight,
the same age as Bobby Jones.
The difference was that Jones retired
because he beat everybody. I retired
because I couldn't beat anybody.

-CHARLES PRICE

The way I hit the ball today, I need to go to the range. Instead, I think I'll go to the bar.

-FUZZY ZOELLER

Waiting to tee off, an Atlanta gentleman spotted a funeral procession going down a nearby road. It was led by a man walking a dog followed by the hearse and about 75 to 80 men in single file. As they passed by, the golfer bowed his head and then asked the man about the strange procession.

"Well, suh," drawled the man, "you see, this is my wife's funeral and she died because this dog bit her."

"I'm terribly sorry for your loss," responded the golfer, "but would you mind if I borrowed the dog for a while?"

"Sure," said the widower, "get in the back of the line."

A very prominent CEO of a very big company was sent this ransom message: "If you ever want to see your wife again, bring $100,000 to the 16th green of Deerfield at eleven o'clock sharp tomorrow." Well, the CEO didn't get there until noon. A masked man jumped out from behind some bushes and snarled, "What took you so long? You're an hour late."

"Hey, cut me some slack," said the CEO. "I have a twenty-five handicap."

The nice thing about these (golf) books is that they usually cancel each other out. One book tells you to keep your eye on the ball; the next says not to bother. Personally, in the crowd I play with, a better idea is to keep your eye on your partner.

-JIM MURRAY

Two old buddies were out on the links on a scorching Wednesday afternoon. On the fifth hole, the first old duffer collapses right on the green. His buddy shouts for help. A pair of doctors playing the fourth hole quickly drive their cart over. One takes out his emergency kit, examines the old guy and says, "I'm sorry, but your friend is dead."

"He was in perfect condition," said the oldster. "That just can't be. I want a second opinion."

With that, the second doctor goes back to his cart, takes out a small cat from his golf bag, and places it near the dead man. The cat sniffs around the man's feet, walks around his body sniffing all the while, and then sits down and begins meowing at the doctor.

"What's that supposed to mean?" asks the old duffer.

"The cat says your friend is dead," responds the doctor.

The man tearfully says, "I can't believe it."

"That'll be three hundred fifty dollars," says the doctor.

"What? I would agree to pay something, but where do you get off charging me three hundred fifty bucks?"

"It's fifty dollars for the diagnosis," replies the doctor, "and three hundred dollars for the cat scan."

If a lot of people gripped a knife and fork the way they do a golf club, they'd starve to death.

-Sam Snead

Take two weeks off and then quit the game.

-JIMMY DEMARET, GIVING ADVICE
TO AN UNHAPPY DUFFER

The hardest shot is a mashie at 90 yards from the green, where the ball has to be played against an oak tree, bounces back into a sand trap, hits a stone, bounces on the green, and then rolls into the cup. The shot is so difficult I have only made it once.

-ZEPPO MARX

Two old golfers were reminiscing as they played. One pointed towards the woods. "My first girlfriend was named Mary Katherine Agnes Colleen Patricia Marion Margaret Kathleen O'Shaugnessey. Back when I was a lad, working as a caddie, I carved her name in one of those trees right over there."

"Whatever happened?" asked his friend.

"The tree fell on me."

A guy went to a psychiatrist and announced, "There's nothing wrong with me, Doc, but my wife says if I don't come see you, she's getting a divorce."

"And exactly what does she think is the matter?" asked the shrink.

"Well," the new patient replied, "you see, I'm Jack Nicklaus and she seems to think there's something wrong with that."

A bit surprised, the psychiatrist asked, "Jack Nicklaus, as in the world-famous golfer?"

"Yep, that's me."

Knowing full well that the patient sitting before him was not Jack Nicklaus, the doctor prescribed three therapy sessions a week.

After two years of this intensive treatment, the psychiatrist announced to his patient, "Congratulations, you're cured."

"Congratulations for what?" grumbled his patient. "Before I came to you, I was Jack Nicklaus. Now I'm a nobody."

If you can smile when all around you have
lost their heads - you must be the caddie.

-ANONYMOUS

A guy walks into the 19th Hole and orders two martinis. The bartender serves them and says, "If it's all the same to you, buddy, I could have made a double and used one glass."

The guy says, "Oh, I know, but my golfing partner died and, just before he did, I promised him I'd order him a drink after each round of golf."

The next week the guy comes back and says to the bartender, "I'll have a martini."

The bartender says, "And one for your buddy, too?"

He says, "Oh, no. This is for my buddy. I'm on the wagon."

A duffer made a terrible shot and, in the process, tore up a gigantic piece of turf. He picked it up, turned to his caddy and said, "What should I do with it?"

The caddy replied, "If I were you, I'd take it home to practice on."

"obSIRvations"

Baseball players quit playing and they play golf. Football players quit, take up golf. What are we supposed to take up when we quit?

-George Archer

Probably I'm a hell of a lot more famous for being the guy who hit the golf ball on the moon than the first guy in space.

-APOLLO 14 ASTRONAUT ALAN SHEPARD

Although golf was originally restricted to wealthy, overweight Protestants, today it's open to anybody who owns hideous clothing.

-DAVE BARRY

Q: *What's the definition of a mulligan?*

A: *The opportunity to repeat a mistake right away.*

~~~~

Q: *What's the easiest golf stroke?*

A: *The fourth putt!*

What's the official drink of the nineteenth hole?
Lilac Crazy.

At his 50th wedding anniversary party held at the local country club, Grandpa Steve was asked the secret of his long marriage. He stood up before his assembled crowd of friends and relatives and shared his marital philosophy.

"Gertrude and I have made it a practice throughout our long marriage to play golf and then go out for two romantic, candlelit dinners a week – right here at this country club. Unfailingly, twice a week, we come here and enjoy the delicious food and soft music. We soak up the ambiance of this fine establishment and sip a vintage wine. She goes Thursdays and I go Fridays."

My God, he looks like he's beating a chicken.

-BYRON NELSON,
ON ACTOR JACK LEMMON'S SWING

Old Cornwaithe was playing alone at Pebble Beach one foggy day when he heard a voice from the nearby water hazard.

"Hey, Mister," the voice said.

He looked around but saw no one so he resumed his slow creak towards the green.

A few seconds later, he heard, "Hey, Mister," once again.

He parted the tall grass at the edge of the water and looked down at a frog perched on a leaf.

The frog said, "Yeah, it's me."

"So what do you want, frog?" the old man wheezed.

"Listen, Mister," the frog replied. "I'm really a beautiful princess but an evil witch has cast a spell upon me and turned me into an ugly, slimy frog. All I need is a kiss and I'll turn back into a gorgeous princess. Pick me up, kiss me and then I'm all yours."

With that, the old man scooped up the frog and slipped her in his golf bag.

"Hey, Mister," the frog protested. "Aren't you going to kiss me? What about all the fun you can have with me?"

"Thanks just the same," Cornwaithe responded, "but at my age, I'd just as soon have a talking frog."

The trouble with playing golf with an Englishman is that every time somebody yells "Fore!" he sits down for tea!

By the time a man can afford to lose a golf ball, he can't hit that far.

-JACOB BRAUDE

I get confused with all the rules in golf.
Let's say you're playing in L.A. and your
ball lands on a dead body. Is your relief one
or two club lengths?

—WENDY MORGAN

A guy runs into the pro shop and yells,
"Quick. Do you know a cure for a terrible case
of hiccups?"

Without saying a word, the pro gives the guy
a swift kick to the stomach, forcing him to gasp
for air.

"I bet you don't have the hiccups now," says
the pro.

"No, but my partner on the first tee does."

A man went to a therapist for a consultation about an obession that was ruining his health. "It's golf, Doc. Golf is destroying me. I'm desperate. I can't even escape it in my sleep. As soon as I close my eyes, I'm out there sinking a two-foot putt or making a magnificent drive right down the fairway. When I wake up in the morning, I'm even more tired than I was before I went to bed. What am I going to do? Can you help me?"

The therapist answered reassuringly, "First of all, you are going to have to make a conscious effort not to dream about golf. For example, when you close your eyes at night, try to imagine something else exciting, like discovering a gold mine or sailing on an around-the-world cruise."

The patient replied, "That's easy for you to say, Doc. If I do that, I'll miss my tee-time."

I asked my instructor how I could cut ten strokes off my score. He told me to quit on hole 17!

-**ARLENE POWERS**

The newcomer to the course was studying the ball and its distance from the green. "What do you think?" he asked the caddie.

"Well, yesterday I caddied for Rodney Dangerfield. He hits 'em about like you. I advised him to use an eight-iron."

With that, the golfer took out his eight-iron, addressed the ball and played his shot– a shot that fell far short of the green.

The angry golfer said, "I thought you told Rodney Dangerfield to use an eight."

"I did. He didn't reach the green either."

"Father," the young man said to the priest, "Is it a sin to play golf on Christmas Day?"

"My son," replied the padre, placing his hand on the fellow's shoulder, "The way you play golf, it's a sin any day."

"obSIRvations"

Golf is the most fun you can have without taking your clothes off.

-Chi Chi Rodriguez

Like a lot of fellows on the Senior Tour, I have a furniture problem. My chest has fallen into my drawers.

-BILLY CASPER

The older you get, the easier it is to shoot your age.

-**JERRY BARBER**

Charlie showed up for an early tee time looking exhausted.

"Hey Charley, what happened?" asked his golfing buddy.

"Oh, I had a big fight with my wife," he replied, still a bit dazed.

"I thought your wife was out of town last night."

"Yeah," Charlie answered ruefully. "So did I."

Harry was playing a short hole when his drive smacked into a bird which fell right into the cup. This marked the first time ever for a partridge in a par three.

Two guys were at the nineteenth hole discussing their golf game.

"This is one heckuva tough course to play," said one of them. "How did you do?"

"Oh, pretty much the same as I always do," replied the second duffer. "I'm a pre-putt-par."

"What's that mean?" asked the other guy.

"It means I shoot par on the fairway and four-putt on the green."

They have some new equipment now that favors seniors. Like that long putter you put right under your chin. You can putt and take a nap at the same time.

-ANONYMOUS

I'm working as hard as I can to get my life
and my cash to run out at the same time.
If I can just die after lunch Tuesday,
everything will be perfect.

-DOUG SANDERS

A guy goes to the doctor for a checkup.
Afterwards, the doctors says, "I've got good news and bad news."

The guy says, "Give me the bad news first, Doc."

"You've got an incurable disease and probably won't live more than a year."

"Geez, what could possibly be the good news?"

"I broke 80 yesterday."

Be honest, caddie," Weinstein said as he teed up his ball on the 18th hole. *"Do you see any change in my game since we started?"*

The caddie stroked his chin thoughtfully for a moment and replied, *"Well sir, they're getting longer."*

"My drives?" asked Weinstein.

"No, sir... our shadows."

Swing hard in case you hit it.

-Dan Marino

I want to win here, stand on the 18th green, and say "I'm going to the World Series."

-LARRY NELSON, ON A
GOLF TOURNAMENT IN DISNEY WORLD

If there were no golf balls,

how would we measure hail?

-ANONYMOUS

Barney's on the 18th hole with two golf balls left, an old one and a new one. His tee shot has to go over a lake and he can't make up his mind which ball to play.

All of the sudden, the clouds part and a heavenly voice bellows, "Have faith. Play the new ball."

Barney can't believe his ears, but he's not about to doubt what he just heard, so he tees up the new ball. Once again, a voice from above roars, "Take a practice swing."

Barney scratches his head, but going along with the divine advice, takes his usual hacker's swing. Just as he's about to hit the ball, the clouds part one more time and the voice says, "Play the old ball!"

Manny, playing in a two-ball foursome, drove his tee shot to the edge of the green on a par three hole. Ralph, playing the second shot, managed to chip it over the green into a bunker.

Undaunted, Manny recovered with a fine shot to within three feet of the hole. Ralph missed the easy putt, leaving Manny to finish the hole.

"Do you realize we took five strokes on an easy par three?" said Manny.

"Yes, and don't forget who took three of them!" replied Ralph.

Gimme: An agreement between two losers who can't putt.

-JIM BISHOP

If you pick up a golfer and hold it to your ear,
like a conch shell, you will hear an alibi.

-FRED BECK

I don't care to join any club that's
prepared to have me as a member.

-Groucho Marx

Irving and Irma were a loving, but very competitive
couple. They also both talked in their sleep. Irving
loved golf and Irma loved auctions.
One night, in the wee small hours, Irving cried out,
"Fore!"

Irma, deep in slumber, snorted and yelled,
"Four-fifty!"

Father Flanagan was playing golf with a parishioner. On the first hole, he sliced his tee shot into the rough. His playing partner heard the priest mutter, "Hoover" under his breath.

On the second hole, his ball went straight into a water hazard. Again, the priest muttered, "Hoover."

He got lucky on the third hole as his tee shot landed on the green. "Praise be to God," exclaimed Father Flanagan.

He lined up his five-foot putt but missed it. "Hoover!" he yelled.

His opponent, now curious about the term, asked why the priest said "Hoover."

Father Flanagan responded, "It's the biggest dam I know."

I'm the best. I just haven't played yet.

-MUHAMMAD ALI

A pastor, doctor and a car dealer were waiting one morning for a particularly slow foursome.

Finally, they became so tired of waiting, waiting and waiting that they sought out the greenskeeper.

The pastor said, "Hey, what's with that group ahead of us? They're slow as molasses."

The greenskeeper responded, "Oh, that's a group of blind firefighters. They lost their sight saving our clubhouse from a fire last year, so we always let them play for free whenever they'd like."

The pastor said, "That's so sad. I'll say a special prayer for them tonight."

The doctor chimed in, "And I'm going to contact my ophthalmologist buddy ... Maybe he can do something for them."

The car dealer complained, "Why can't these guys play at night?"

The manager of the pro shop was confused about paying an invoice for some golf gear. Not exactly an Einstein at math, he asked his secretary for some help. "If I were to give you $15,000 minus 12%, how much would you take off?"

She answered, "Everything but my earrings."

"obSIRvations"

One of the advantages bowling has
over golf is that you seldom lose a
bowling ball.

-Don Carter

*The score a player reports on any hole should
always be regarded as his opening offer.*

-THOMAS MULLIGAN

GOLFER'S HOROSCOPE

Aquarius (Jan 20-Feb 18) The Golf Club

Born under the sign of the country club, you are industrious, prosperous and like to wear funny pants. Your idea of excitement is pulling the old "dead mouse in the golfbag" trick on the newest member of the club.

Pisces (Feb 19-Mar 20) The Sand Trap

You are a Child of The Sand Trap. You are innately drawn to the rough and to water hazards. This is because in a former life, you were either Lewis or Clark.

Aries (Mar 21-Apr 19) The Golf Tee

Born under the sign of the tee, you came into the world along with the spring- which explains why the smell of newly mowed grass follows you everywhere. It's all those divots!

Taurus (Apr 20-May 20) The Golf Ball

Born under the sign of the golfball, you tend to be round and dimpled all over.

Gemini (May 21-Jun 21) The Golf Swing

Like all Gemini golfers, you have a tendency to stand too close to the ball. Unfortunately, that's also true after you've hit it.

Cancer (Jun 22-Jul 22) The 19th Hole

The summer heat means that you are one of the chosen children of the 19th Hole. Trading golfballs for highballs, you play a round then buy one.

GOLFER'S HOROSCOPE

Leo (Jul 23-Aug 22) The Driving Range

Your life is intimately tied up with the game. Sadly, the best drive you'll ever make is in a golf cart.

Virgo (Aug 23-Sep 22) The Scorecard

A Scorecardian, you are good with numbers...a talent you put to good use in cheating.

Libra (Sep 23-Oct 23) The Water Hazard

Under the sign of the Water Hazard you are forever losing your ball in the drink. You have such an amazing ability at finding the water that your golfing companions refer to your woods as "diving sticks."

Scorpio (Oct 24-Nov 21) The Golf Shoe

You are tremendously gifted at golf. In fact, you immediately master any hole you attempt... especially the ones with windmills.

Sagittarius (Nov 22-Dec 21) The Glove

Though your tee off time is late in the year, you are devoted to your sport. This is a shame because, basically, you stink!

Capricorn (Dec 22-Jan 19) The Fairway

Though you have much power, you are horribly inconsistent. In fact, you would do well to hit your first drive before deciding which course you'll be playing that day.

Tiger Woods? I thought that was a golf course.

-SANDY LYLE,
ON THEN JUNIOR GOLF STAR TIGER WOODS

The word of the heroic deed had spread all over the country club. All the members were asking Irving about his Herculean effort in carrying his stricken partner back to the clubhouse for treatment.

"I can't believe Riley had a heart attack right in the middle of a game!" said one as he sipped his drink in the clubhouse.

"Yeah – and Riley must weigh what– 300 pounds? How did you ever manage to lift him over your shoulder and carry him back, Irving?"

"Well," said Irving, basking in the glory, "carrying him was nothing. It was picking him up and putting him down at every stroke that was the hard part."

An aggressive salesman was at a restaurant with an important customer when he spotted Arnold Palmer dining across the room. Aware that his client was a golf nut, he figured he'd try to score some points. The salesman excused himself, went over to Palmer's table and said, "Pardon me, Mr. Palmer, but I've got a gigantic business deal in the works. My customer is a big fan of yours. If you'd stop by my table and just say, 'Hi, Joe,' this could put me over the top."

Palmer nodded his head and went back to his meal. When he finished, he went over to the salesman's table, tapped him on the back and said, "Hi, Joe."

Without looking up, the salesman snapped back, "Later, Arnie. Can't you see I'm eating?"

If it weren't for golf, I'd probably be a caddie today.

-GEORGE ARCHER

The rest of the field.

-ROGER MALTBIE,
ON WHAT HE HAD TO SHOOT TO WIN

Q: *What do you call it when a T-rex breaks even in golf?*

A: *Jurassic Par*

An expectant mother who was a couple of weeks overdue was told by her doctor to walk as much as possible every morning until the baby came. The M.D. also advised her husband that he should go along just in case anything started.

"Alright, Doc," replied the husband. "But would it be okay if she carries my clubs while she walks?"

Did you hear about the divorce lawyer who did a mailing to all the married male members of the exclusive country club?

She sent out 175 Valentines signed "Guess who?"

Golf and women are a lot alike. You know you are not going to wind up with anything but grief, but you can't resist the impulse.

-Jackie Gleason

I can't wait until we make an eagle.

-CHI CHI RODRIGUEZ, TALKING ABOUT HIS ATTRACTIVE PARTNER IN A MIXED-PAIRS TOURNAMENT WHO GAVE HIM A KISS EACH TIME THEY BIRDIED

The Senior Tour is like a class reunion.
It's the same as it was 30 years ago.
We tell the same dirty jokes only they're
funnier now.

-BOB TOSKI

And then there was the guy whose doctor advised him to play 36 holes a day so he went out and bought a harmonica.

Q: Why is golf a lot like taxes?
A: You drive very hard to get to the green only to wind up in a hole.

Two golfers are standing on the 10th tee. Jerry takes about 20 practice swings, changes his grip five or six times, and adjusts his stance just as much.

"Hey, Jerry! Play, for heaven's sake. We don't have all day," says Chris.

"Hold on a minute, I gotta do this right. See the woman standing up there on the clubhouse porch? That's my mother-in-law and I would like to get off the perfect shot," says Jerry.

Chris looks, and about 250 yards away he sees the woman.

"You must be kidding. You couldn't possibly hit her from here."

I believe my future is ahead of me.

-CHIP BECK, AFTER HIS FIRST PGA TOUR WIN

Harry the hacker was teeing off on the sixteenth hole of Pinehurst when he died of a sudden heart attack. The next thing you know, he stood before St. Peter at the Pearly Gates. "Welcome to heaven, Harry," said St. Peter. "Come, let me show you around the place."

St. Peter led Harry to a variety of beautiful places, including some of the best golf courses he'd ever laid eyes on. At one point, St. Peter brought Harry into a gigantic room with clocks all over the walls. "What are all these clocks for?" asked Harry.

St. Peter replied, "Ah, these are actually profanity dial indicators for all the golfers who've joined us this year. The more a golfer cussed on the links, the faster the hands move."

"Wow," said Harry. "Where's mine?"

"Sorry to report that they're using yours as a fan for the family room."

Then there was the hunter who got a hole-in-one but went crazy trying to figure out how to mount it.

The most exquisitely satisfying act in the world of golf is that of throwing a club. The full backswing, the delayed wrist action, the flowing follow-through, followed by that unique whirring sound, reminiscent only of a passing flock of starlings, are without parallel in sport.

-Henry Longhurst

Hold up a one-iron and walk. Even God can't hit a one-iron.

**-LEE TREVINO,
ON HOW TO DEAL WITH LIGHTNING**

The guy was a first rate on-the-course and off-the-course louse.

When he died, he went to Hell. His eternal punishment was to serve as a caddie for the Devil. This was not your normal golf bag toting duty. The Devil plays with a hot hand...oven-heated golf clubs and balls.

Just as the guy is prepared to caddie for the first time in Hell, he sees a former playing partner, a hideously ugly man, on the first tee with a beautiful woman.

The eternally damned caddie mutters out loud, "Why do I have to suffer like this when that guy gets to spend his time with a gorgeous woman like that?"

The Devil hears him and says, "Who do you think you are to question that woman's punishment?"

Sam and Moe were rocking on the porch of the palatial Miami country club after enjoying a round of golf.

Having talked about everything under the sun during their many games together, Sam was grasping for a new topic of conversation.

"Tell me, Moe, have you read Marx?" Sam asked.

"Yes," replied Moe. "And, you know, I think it's the wicker chairs."

It's nice to look down the fairway and see your mother on the left and your father on the right. You know that no matter whether you hook it or slice it, somebody is going to be there to kick it back in the fairway.

-LARRY NELSON

It takes Latinos nine hours to play golf. Four hours for eighteen holes, and five hours to do the lawn.

-GEORGE LOPEZ

The golfer's ball landed in a thicket of weeds in the middle of some woods, an unplayable lie if ever there was one. He tried to line it up but realized it was futile so he picked the ball up and moved it to a better position, shouting to his playing partners, "Found it." Suddenly, he had the feeling he was being watched. He turned around and saw an escaped convict whose picture had been plastered all over the newspaper.

The two men looked at each other for a long moment, then the golfer whispered, "Shhhh. I won't tell if you don't."

Tom runs excitedly into the locker room and holds up a golf ball. "Look at this!" he says.

"Looks like a plain old golf ball to me," says Steve.

"This is no ordinary golf ball," Tom responds. "This is a golf ball that can not be lost."

Steve says, "Yeah, sure. Any ball can be lost."

"Not this one," replies Tom. "It's got a special radar tracking device so that if you hit it in the woods or rough or even the water, you can locate it."

"Oh yeah? Where'd you get this super-duper ball, anyway?"

"I found it."

You've got just one problem. You stand too close to the ball - after you've hit it.

-SAM SNEAD

Golf is so popular because it is the best game in the world at which to be bad ... At golf, it is the bad player who gets the most strokes.

-A.A. MILNE

In golf, when we hit a foul ball, we've got to go out and play it.

-Sam Snead, *comparing golf to baseball*

Lonnie: I'll never play golf with my banker again.

Terry: Why not?

Lonnie: Every time I yell "Fore," he yells "Closure."

Harry was going by a large and deep bunker when he heard muffled cries for help. Peering down into the trap, he saw his buddy *Larry* trapped under an overturned golf cart.

"I think my leg is broken," groaned *Larry*.

"Does our lawyer know you're here?" called *Harry*.

"No, nobody does."

"Great," said *Larry*, climbing down into the trap. "Move over."

You know you're getting old when all the names in your black book have M.D. after them.

-**Arnold Palmer**

The winds were blowing 50 mph and gusting to 70. I hit a par 3 with my hat.

-CHI CHI RODRIGUEZ,
ON A WINDY COURSE IN SCOTLAND

Two duffers were playing a round in Florida. The first one went off to find his ball in the rough while the second guy hopped in the cart and drove to the fairway. Minutes went by and there was no sign of the golfer in the rough, so his buddy hopped back in the cart to find his friend. He arrived on the scene to see his friend buried up to his waist in quicksand and sinking fast. "Stay still. I'll go get a rope to pull you out," said the second golfer.

"Forget about that! Quick – bring me a sand wedge!"

Four old golfers took to the links on a Saturday morning as they had every week for the past ten years. The competition was as keen as ever.

On the sixth hole, one of the golfers suddenly collapsed just as he was about to hit a bunker shot. As he lay on the ground, one of the other golfers shouted, "I think Nellie just had a stroke."

Said another player, "Well, just make sure he marks it on his card."

"obSIRvations"

Golf is a game of expletives not deleted.

-Dr. Irving A. Gladstone

You know this is the Senior Tour when your back goes out more than you do.

-Bob Bruce

Golfers are the only athletes who must dive through hundreds of spectators while in the middle of a game. It's like allowing fans to come out of the football stadium and ask for Joe Namath's autograph between plays.

-DAN SIKES

"Golf, golf, golf. That's all you ever think about," griped the newlywed bride at the dinner table. "You've been on the golf course every single day of our honeymoon."

"Sweetheart," cooed her husband in his most soothing tone as he reached across the table to take her hand. "Believe me, golf is the last thing on my mind at this moment. Now please stop this silliness and let's get back to our meal. Would you please pass the putter?"

A foreign spaceship hovered over a golf course and two aliens watched a lone duffer in amazement. The golfer hit his tee shot into the rough, took three shots to get back on the fairway, sliced the next one into the woods, and then took two to get back on the fairway again.

Meanwhile, one alien told the other that he must be playing some sort of weird game and they continued to watch in fascination.

The golfer then hit a shot into a bunker by the green. A few shots later, he made it onto the green. He four-putted to finally get into the hole. At this juncture, the other alien said to his partner, "Wow! Now he's in serious trouble!"

Golf is not a sport. It's men in ugly pants, walking.

-ROSIE O'DONNELL

I'm into golf now. I'm getting pretty good.
I can almost hit the ball as far as I can
throw the clubs.

-**Bob Ettinger**

If you drink, don't drive. Don't even putt.

-Dean Martin

Gale: *Played golf with my boss the other day.*

Howard: *How'd it go?*

Gale: *Well, on the first hole, the boss topped the*
ball and only sent it about 20 feet, leaving it
375 yards from the hole.

Howard: *What'd you do?*

Gale: *I conceded the putt.*

Q: *What type of engine do they use in golf carts?*
A: *Fore cylinder.*

Standing on the tee of a long par three, the confident golfer said to his caddie, "Looks like a four-wood and a putt to me."

The caddie handed him the four-wood with which the golfer topped the ball about 15 yards in front of the tee. Immediately, the caddie handed him his putter and said, "And now for one heck of a putt."

Never have so many spent so much to sit in relative comfort to brag about their failures.

-KEITH JACKSON

The reason the pro tells you to keep your
head down is so you can't see him laughing.

-PHYLLIS DILLER

Then there was the bachelor who preferred golf to women. But he finally found the love of his life and got married. You might say he learned to put his heart before the course.

Golfer: I think I'm going to drown myself
       in the lake.

Caddie: Think you can keep your head down
       that long?

Barrington: I say, did you hear what happened to Rockingham?

Hyde-White: No, I'm afraid I haven't.

Barrington: He was awakened in the middle of the night by a burglar and beat the miscreant into submission with a five-iron.

Hyde-White: Do tell. How many strokes?

Golf is much more fun than walking naked in a strange place, but not much.

-Buddy Hackett

I like to say I was born on the nineteenth hole - the only hole I ever parred.

-GEORGE LOW

I played so bad, I got a get-well card from the IRS.

-JOHNNY MILLER

Fred, playing as a single, was teamed with a twosome. Eventually, they asked why he was playing by himself on such a beautiful day.

"My dear wife and I played this course together for over thirty years but this year she passed away. I kept the tee time in her memory."

The twosome were touched at the thoughtfulness of the gesture but one asked him why no one from among her friends and family was willing to take her spot.

"Oh," responded Fred, "they're all at the funeral."

Bentley took a series of giant steps as he stepped out of the cart and made his way to the first green. "What the heck was that all about?" questioned his partner.

"Well," answered Bentley, "my wife told me that if I want to play tomorrow, it'll be over her dead body, so I'm practicing."

Maybe you've heard about the duffer who's so bad he has an unplayable lie when he tees up.

The reason most people play golf is to wear clothes they would not be caught dead in otherwise.

-ROGER SIMON

One day on the links a man was separated from his companions for a few moments and the devil took the opportunity to appear to him. "Say, friend," the devil said in his best used car salesman smile, "how'd you like to make a hole-in-one to impress your buddies?"

"What's the catch?" asked the fellow suspiciously.

"It'll shorten your love life by five years," grinned the devil.

"Hmmm. All right, I'll do it," agreed the man.

He then went on to make one of the most spectacular shots ever and aced the hole. A few minutes later the devil approached the man on the following tee. "How'd you like to go for two in a row?"

"At what cost?" asked the man.

"This'll shorten your love life by ten years."

"You drive a tough bargain, but okay," replied the golfer who strode to the tee and sent a 310 yard beauty right into the cup.

At the next tee, the devil appeared once again. "This

is a once in a lifetime offer. If you ace this one, it'll be three straight holes-in-one. It's never been done before in the history of the world. But it's gonna cost you another 20 years off your love life."

"Let's go for it," said the man who proceeded to dazzle everyone by hitting the ball from behind his back, sending it over a huge pond onto the green and right into the hole.

It was such an amazing shot that even the devil himself applauded. And that's how Father O'Malley got into the Guinness Book of World Records.

I'm not an intellectual person. I don't get headaches from concentration. I get them from double bogies.

                                        -TOM WEISKOPF

There are no mulligans in that sport.

-GARY PLAYER, ON BUNGEE JUMPING

Baseball reveals character; golf exposes it.

-Baseball Hall of Famer Ernie Banks

On the tenth hole, a foursome was getting ready to tee off when a man came running up to them completely out of breath.

"I say old chaps, I hate to interrupt but I've just gotten word that my wife has fallen seriously ill."

"Bad break old boy," replied one of the men. "Is there anything at all we can do?"

"Well, if you don't mind, you could let me play through."

Did you hear about the Siamese twins who wrote a book about their golfing experiences? It's called Tee for Two.

~~~~

Then there was the dyslexic duffer who always wondered how to flog.

~~~~

The duffer walks into the pro shop and says, "Pete, what can I do to lower my handicap?"

Pete the pro says, "Here, take this."

"But this is just a pencil."

"Yes, but it has an eraser attached."

Did you know John Daly hit a tee shot -
and two tracking stations picked it up
as a satellite?

-JIM MURRAY

Be funny on a golf course? Do I kid my best friend's mother about her heart condition?

-PHIL SILVERS

"obSIRvations"

It's so ridiculous to see a golfer with a one-foot putt and everybody is saying "Shhh" and not moving a muscle. Then we allow 19-year-old kids to face a game-deciding free throw with 17,000 people yelling.

-Al McGuire

They were at the 19th Hole, watching the live telecast of the British Open when someone says, "Turn up the sound."

Someone else says, "Ssssh...not while Faldo is putting."

A guy applies for a sales position with a big golf equipment manufacturer. While he's waiting for the interview, the receptionist tells him, "You seem like a nice guy. Let me give you a tip. My boss is very sensitive about the fact that he doesn't have any ears. At some point, he's going to ask you if you notice anything odd about him. Whatever you do, don't make any mention of the ears."

The guy thanks the receptionist for the advice and goes in for the interview. Well, the boss is very impressed with the guy's resume, his knowledge of the game in general and of golf gear in particular. But sure enough, at one point the boss says, "Tell me. Do you notice anything different about me?"

The guy looks at the boss and responds, "Well, now that you mention it, I can tell you're wearing contact lenses."

"That's amazing. I like perceptiveness in my employees. But how on earth did you know I wear contacts?"

"Easy. You'd be wearing glasses if you had any ears."

*Give me golf clubs, the fresh air, and a
beautiful partner, and you can keep my
golf clubs and the fresh air.*

-JACK BENNY

Terry and Joe were teeing off early one summer's day when the usual tranquility of the golf course was shattered by the siren of an ambulance racing to the maternity hospital atop a nearby hill.

"Somebody's getting a big surprise today," remarked Joe.

"I'll say," replied Terry as he lined up his putt. "When I left this morning, my wife's contractions were still at least an hour apart."

A very attractive but ill-intended young woman made it a practice to hang around the exclusive country club looking to settle down with a very rich and very old man. She found her man in J.P. Fotheringham, the 92 year-old financier. Sure enough, she and J.P. tied the knot.

Within months, J.P. became ill. As his condition worsened, the old duffer was advised to make a new will. He asked his wife, "Honey, what should I do about my estate?"

She gently hugged him and cooed, "J.P., I think you should leave all of your worldly possessions to your greatest source of comfort."

Just a few days after his rewritten will was made, the old man died. At the reading of his will, his wife learned that he left 20 million dollars to his country club.

The woods are full of long hitters.

-HARVEY PENICK

Taking some well deserved time off from their heavenly duties, Moses and St. Peter hit the links to indulge themselves in a game of golf. Moses teed up and hit a beautiful shot right down the fairway to the green about two feet from the hole. St. Peter, however, whacked a bad hook which disappeared into the woods. Moses was smiling smugly when an eagle emerged from high over a nearby Interstate and dropped the ball into the exhaust stack of a passing tractor-trailor. The pressure buildup soon shot the ball back into the air where it was struck by lightning from some low-lying clouds. That sent the ball careening off several chimneys and it ricocheted right back to the golf course, landed on the green and rolled right into the hole. Moses sighed, turned to a smiling St. Peter and said, "Oh, c'mon- not when we're playing for money!"

Q: How many golfers does it take to screw in a light bulb?

A: Two. One to do it and another to tell him he looked up.

If you call on God to improve the results of a shot while it is still in motion, you are using "an outside agency" and subject to appropriate penalties under the rules of golf.

-Henry Longhurst

Being left-handed is a big advantage.
No one knows enough about your swing to mess you up with advice.

-BOB CHARLES

Would you believe there are 3,000 miniature golf courses in the city of Los Angeles? Half of America is bent over.

—WILL ROGERS

Q: Why did the golfer want to live to be 125?

A: Just once he wanted to be able to shoot his age.

~~~~

Q: What's a golfer's favorite soft drink?

A: Slice.

~~~~

Q: What did the ancient Romans yell on the golf course?

A: "IV!"

Bismo the Gorilla was making a fortune for his owner. They'd travel around to golf courses and challenge the pro to a round of golf. They always accepted the bet figuring that they could easily beat the muscle-bound primate. That was, until Bismo stepped up to the tee and drove the ball 450 yards. Then they'd usually give up, pay the bet and scamper away with their tails between their legs.

One morning, a top-rated country club pro conceded the bet after the gorilla drove the ball 450 yards to the green.

"Just out of curiosity," the pro asked as he forked over the cash, "how does Bismo putt?"

"The same as he drives," said the gorilla's owner. "450 yards."

Real golfers don't cry when they line up their fourth putt.

-KAREN HURWITZ

Tiger Woods goes into the nineteenth hole and spots Stevie Wonder. "Hey, Stevie, it's Tiger. How's your singing career doing these days?"

"I can't complain. How are you hitting 'em?"

Woods responds, "My swing is going real well right now."

Stevie says, "Mine, too."

"What? You play golf?" asks Tiger.

"Sure … I've been playing for years," replies Stevie.

"But you're blind," Woods says. "How can you possibly play?"

Wonder replies, "I get my caddy to stand in the middle of the fairway and holler to me. When I hear the sound of his voice, I play the ball toward him. Then, after I get to where the ball lands, the caddy moves down to the green and again I play the ball toward his voice."

"But how do you putt?" asks Tiger.

"Simple ... My caddy lies down in front of the hole and calls to me with his head on the ground. And then I play the ball toward his voice," explains Stevie.

"What's your handicap, Stevie?"

Stevie responds, "I'm a scratch golfer."

Woods says, "We've got to play a round sometime."

"Sure, but people don't take me seriously, so I only play for money – and never for less than $5,000 a hole."

"You're on. When would you like to play?" asks Woods.

Stevie says, "Pick a night."

A golfer is someone with hoof and mouth disease. He hoofs it all day and mouths it all night.

-WILL ROGERS

Some guys hope to shoot their age. Craig
Stadler hopes to shoot his waist.

-JIM MURRAY

The phone at the pro shop rang and was answered by the young clerk.

"These $300 shoes you sold me are too tight," complained the voice at the other end.

"Well, sir, for a shoe to fit properly, you have to make sure the tongue is pulled all the way out."

"Okay, but deth stilth feel awfulth tightth."

"Why do you keep looking at your watch?" the annoyed duffer asked his caddy.

"It's not a watch, sir. It's a compass."

A man tees up at the first hole. All of a sudden, a woman wearing a bridal gown comes running toward him. "You bum! You bum!" she screams.

"Aw, c'mon, dear," he says. "I told you only if it rains."

Golf appeals to the idiot in us and the child. What child does not grasp the pleasure principle of miniature golf? Just how childlike golf players become is proven by their frequent inability to count past five.

                                                                    -John Updike

Even the men's room has a double dogleg.

                                          -DAVE STOCKTON, ON THE
                                          POPPY HILLS GOLF COURSE

*My golf is getting better all the time. Today
I parred all but sixteen holes.*

-WENDY MORGAN

Man, that Wally cheats," grumbled the golfer.

"Why do you say that?" his buddy asked.

*"Today on the fourth hole, he lost his ball in the
rough and slyly played a new one."*

"How do you know?"

"Because I had his original ball in my pocket."

*Of course you've heard about the foursome that
was so bad they called themselves 'The Bronchitis
Brothers' because they were just a bunch of hackers.*